Wembley Stadium

£4

The Deutsche Bibliothek holds
a record for this publication in the
Deutsche Nationalbibliografie;
detailed bibliographical data can
be found under http://dnb.ddb.de

Library of Congress Control
Number is available

Prestel Verlag, A Member
of Verlagsgruppe Random
House GmbH

Prestel Verlag
Neumarkter Str. 28
81673 Munich
Germany
Tel   +49 (0)89 4136-0
Fax +49 (0)89 4136-2335
www.prestel.de

Prestel Publishing
900 Broadway, Suite 603
New York NY 10003
USA
Tel   +1 (212) 995-2720
Fax +1 (212) 995-2733

Prestel Publishing Ltd
4 Bloomsbury Place
London
WC1A 2QA
UK
Tel   +44 (020) 7323-5004
Fax +44 (020) 7636-8004
www.prestel.com

ISBN 978-3-7913-4688-5

Wembley Stadium Foster + Partners

Norman Foster
Simon Inglis

PRESTEL
MUNICH · LONDON · NEW YORK

gateway
promise
celebration
permanence

Reflective during the day, a symbol day & Night.

glistening at Night on the skyline, a jewel, a tiara!

WEMBLEY

Extracts from Norman Foster's early Wembley sketches. Here Foster begins to outline ideas for a landmark building, with a triumphal arch – a strong symbol for the new stadium, glistening at night on the skyline, 'a jewel, a tiara' – and explains how the retractable roof allows sunlight to fall on the pitch.

the crown

Partial crown

Tiara

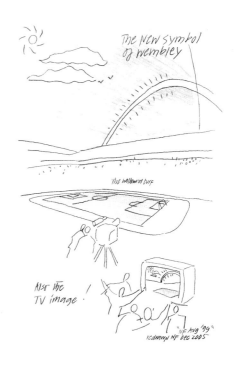

The new symbol of wembley

The hallowed turf

Also the TV image !

"NF Aug '99"
redrawn NF Dec 2005

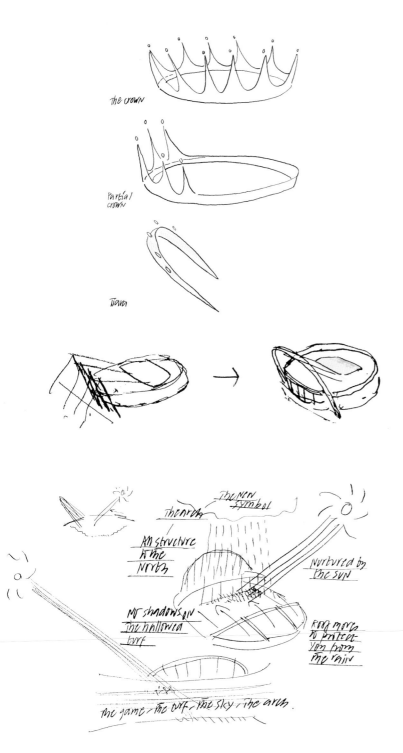

The new symbol

The arch

An structure to the north

Nurtured by the sun

No shadows on the hallowed turf

Roof moves to protection from the rain

the game . the turf . the sky . the arch .

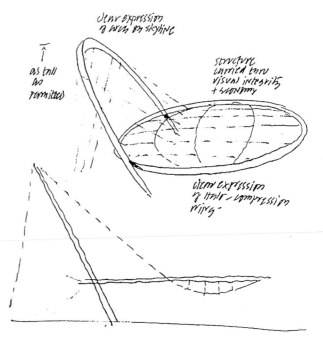

clear expression of arch on skyline

as tall as permitted

structure carried thru visual integrity + economy

clear expression of tensile - compression ring -

5

Introduction Norman Foster

The original Empire Stadium at Wembley was one of the wonders of its age. The focal point of the 1924 British Empire Exhibition, it was designed by Sir John Simpson and Maxwell Ayrton and engineered by Sir Owen Williams. Described at its opening as 'the greatest arena in the world', it was also one of the largest, holding 120,000 mostly standing spectators. The stadium was pioneering in being built entirely from concrete and remarkable for being completed in just 300 days. Over time, it became an international symbol for excellence – the stadium where every footballer in the world aspired to play.

Our involvement with Wembley dates back to 1995, when we were commissioned to create a masterplan for Wembley Stadium, with Brent Council, in response to the Sports Council competition that would decide the location of a new English National Stadium. In 1996, as a result of that competition, Wembley was selected over sites in four other English cities.

As we began to think about the form of the stadium we decided we should consult HOK – the leading stadium designers in the United States – and LOBB, who had designed Stadium Australia and the Millennium Stadium in Cardiff. We eventually decided to work together on the project and subsequently submitted to become architects of the stadium itself.

The client for the new stadium was the newly established English National Stadium Development Company, later to become Wembley National Stadium Limited (WNSL). Delighted at winning the competition, we decided to call ourselves the World Stadium Team.

The first questions we asked ourselves as a team were: what constitutes the best of its kind in the world today; how can we create a new generation stadium; how can we learn from previous stadiums; and what form does such a building take? Beyond its performance as a stadium, the project also had to be conceptually robust enough to withstand many other challenges – political and financial – though we did not know that when we began.

The old Wembley was steeped in memories: from the Olympics of 1948, the Cooper versus Clay fight of 1963, the World Cup Final of 1966, to the Live Aid concert of 1985. My own recollections are from the 1996 European Football Championship and the England semi-final against Germany. That was the final set-piece international game in the old stadium and the last time I experienced the buzz of being there at such an emotionally charged event.

However, putting to one side all the nostalgia about the old stadium, it is worth remembering what it was like in terms of amenities – it was under-serviced, cramped and uncomfortable. Toilet provision, for example, was extremely poor, with only 360 WCs to serve a capacity crowd of 78,000. This compares with 2,600 toilets in the new stadium. The only part of the stadium where hospitality areas were provided was the section between the two towers – the rest was mostly engineering infrastructure – which meant that there was little or no room to improve facilities. The location of an athletics track around the pitch and the very shallow nature of the seating bowl also distanced spectators from the game. Added to that, access to the upper seating rows was difficult and sightlines were poor, with structure blocking views in many areas.

The challenge in reinventing Wembley was to build on its heritage and yet create a venue that would be memorable in its own right. We focused attention on how we could maintain the atmosphere and other special qualities of the old stadium. For example, we undertook acoustic studies to ensure that we could recreate the 'Wembley roar'. Other traditions, such as the route up to the Royal Box to collect the trophy, have also been continued. Originally thirty-nine steps, the route is now 107 steps, located at a pivotal point on the tiers. We also wanted to retain the flexibility to host major concerts and other events, for which Wembley had become famous.

A crucial consideration for football was how to bring people closer to the action on the pitch. The geometry of the seating bowl ensures that everyone has an unobstructed view of the game; and the highest tiers are easily accessed via escalators. At the same time, space standards have improved dramatically. All 90,000 spectators now have the same seating room as only those in the Royal Box enjoyed before.

Beyond the arena itself, the stadium is designed to maximise spectator enjoyment. The outer concourse that wraps around the building allows step-free access into the stadium for all. Hospitality areas can cater for up to 10,000 seated diners simultaneously. In total, the stadium has some two million square feet of facilities – the equivalent of three Swiss Re towers. Interestingly, the British Empire Exhibition provided the equivalent amount of exhibition space spread over 87 hectares, whereas here it is integrated within one compact building form.

One of the key design generators for the stadium was the 'hallowed turf'. Without sunlight and fresh air the grass cannot be maintained in first-class condition. The question was how to protect all 90,000 spectators from the rain, but still allow air and sunlight to reach the pitch. We were acutely aware of the problems other large roofed stadiums had in this respect. The answer was a partially retractable roof, which operates as a series of sliding panels that can be moved to let in the sun, or closed to cover the entire seating bowl.

When we originally launched the scheme this roof was supported by four slender masts. It was a very elegant, logical response. However, I felt instinctively that it wasn't special to Wembley. The day after the press conference at which the scheme was revealed – a Saturday – I was in Bayreuth for the opera festival. I am a passionate cyclist and it was on a cycle ride in the countryside that I decided we had to do better. That is when the arch was conceived.

Over the course of that weekend there was a frantic exchange of sketches by fax between me and Alistair Lenczner – a structural engineer in our London studio. I sketched the arch's potential to be a triumphal symbol for the new stadium and to liberate views along Olympic Way. Alistair investigated the geometry of the arch and how it could be built. Remarkably, he anticipated its eventual height to within a metre.

On Monday morning our model shop made a sketch model, which we showed to Rod Sheard of HOK. He was immediately supportive. Next we had to convince our client, Ken Bates, the chairman of the Football Association. I took a sheaf of my sketches to show him. He saw the benefits straight away, but asked about the cost implication. I reassured him that there was none and he said 'let's do it.'

Interestingly, that same weekend in Bayreuth, I was talking about Wembley and explaining how the quality of the finishes would be as good as the average opera house. Quite rightly the person I was speaking to said: 'Why not? This is a cultural building in every sense.' If you look at the accommodation, from the hospitality suites to the players' changing rooms, you find standards more usually associated with an exclusive hotel or a spa. In fact the business strategy for the stadium was borrowed from the airline industry, which makes 80 per cent of its profits from 20 per cent of its customers. The corporate hospitality boxes in this scenario function like the first-class section of a 747.

In capital terms, the project compares very favourably with a range of European stadiums, which have nothing like the facilities that Wembley offers. The final cost of the building – that is the hardware – was £352 million. If you analyse that figure in terms of cost per seat, it works out at £3,900 per place, while stadiums of this complexity in North America or Japan typically exceed the £4,000-per-seat threshold. Despite that, a huge amount of misinformation about cost was propagated by the press. For example, many people believe that the taxpayer was the client. The reality is that a grant from the National Lottery paid for the purchase of the old stadium and its land; the development of the new stadium was funded entirely by private investment.

As the project progressed it also became a political football. There was pressure, for example, to incorporate a permanent athletics track to meet the Lottery conditions that the new stadium should be able to host athletics events from time to time. However, the experience of the old stadium revealed how unsatisfactory that was for football. We looked at alternatives, such as a retractable tier of seating, but that tends to compromise the upper tiers. Added to that, the likelihood of an international athletics event, such as an Olympiad, being staged at Wembley was once in a lifetime. Our solution was to take a datum from the vomitories in the lower tier and install a temporary deck at that level on to which a track can be laid. In such a scenario the stadium would seat 72,000 people and meet all IAAF technical requirements.

For a project like Wembley to succeed, we absolutely needed a personality like Ken Bates as client. Time and again he made the crucial decisions and stood by them. The same is true of the chairman of Multiplex, John Roberts, who undertook to build the stadium but sadly did not live to see it completed.

Without these two key figures the project would simply not have happened. On behalf of the team I must also pay tribute to WNSL and the FA as clients for their support and patronage.

Seven years after the bulldozers moved in to demolish what was once described as 'the cathedral of football', 90,000 people filled the new stadium for the first FA Cup Final to be played there. Watching that game, I realised that the skill in designing a stadium isn't just the technical detail – although that's hugely important – it's creating a building that bottles emotion. Looking up, you see the arch soaring 133 metres above the pitch. Floodlit at night, it is even more distinctive – an instantly recognisable landmark, visible on the skyline from the heart of the capital.

In retrospect, as our first built stadium, Wembley was something of a learning curve. But in the year that it opened, the knowledge we had gained allowed us to be selected as architects to recast Barcelona's Camp Nou Stadium. More recently we won the commission to design the Lusail Stadium in Qatar, which was proposed as the centrepiece of Qatar's ultimately successful bid for the 2022 FIFA World Cup Final. That stadium should allow us to build on what we gained from Wembley and do something special for the next football generation.

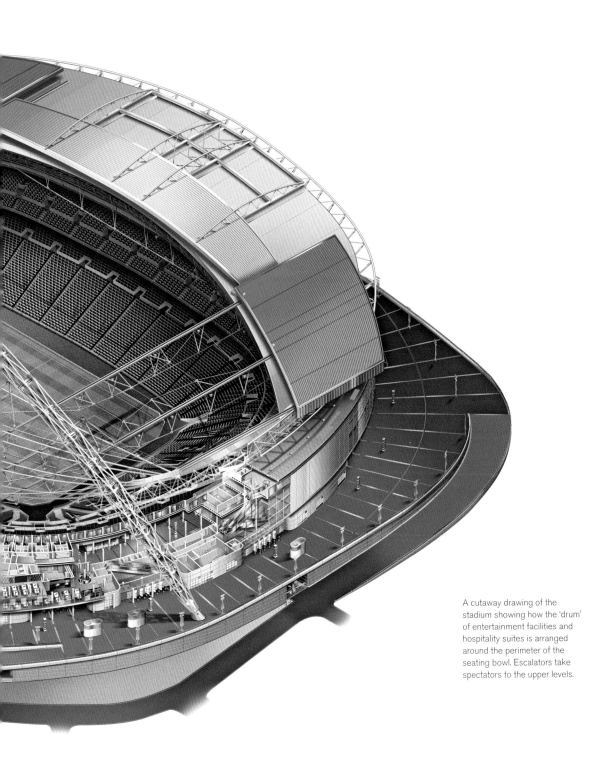

A cutaway drawing of the stadium showing how the 'drum' of entertainment facilities and hospitality suites is arranged around the perimeter of the seating bowl. Escalators take spectators to the upper levels.

Reinventing Wembley Simon Inglis

As a venue for football and concerts, as a profitable commercial operation, but more especially as a construct in the popular imagination, the old Wembley Stadium held a place in world sport virtually unrivalled by any other venue. It was the one commission every stadium architect longed to secure. But it was also one that came heavily laden with issues and constraints. Glorified for its place in footballing history, it was itself the ultimate political football. So when it came to rebuilding Wembley Stadium, it was inevitable that Norman Foster and his colleagues would take on far more than a mere design brief.

From its inaugural match in April 1923, when a crowd of 200,000 overwhelmed the stadium – famously requiring the efforts of a white police horse, Billy, to clear the pitch – Wembley made headlines. Simply in its role as the venue for English football's annual showcase, the FA Cup Final, a match first contested in 1872 and today watched by a television audience of some 400 million, Wembley garnered for itself a unique aura, as an El Dorado of passion, escapism and symbol of national identity.

To the Cup Final must be added Wembley's hosting of the 1948 Olympics, the 1966 World Cup Final, the Live Aid concert of 1985, and the 1996 European Championship. Woven into this narrative may be added countless other historic moments. Thus in the iconography of twentieth-century Britain, the name Wembley transcended its locational identity, becoming, like those other London institutions, 'the City', 'the Palace' or 'the West End,' as much an abstract notion as a physical entity.

Significantly, Wembley was also always a neutral venue. Unlike the majority of countries where the national stadium hosts at least one football club, Wembley has never had a resident team. For most club supporters, therefore, a visit to the old Wembley was often a once-in-a-lifetime event.

For followers of the England team, Wembley represented the nation's fortress, while for overseas players it was the stadium in which they most aspired to play. As the legendary Brazilian, Pelé, commented in 1995: 'Wembley is the cathedral of football, it is the capital of football, and it is the heart of football.' But churches crumble, capitals fall and hearts grow weak, and in reality, in its final years the old Wembley had become a national embarrassment as a venue. Only its emblematic twin towers inspired any real affection.

Especially deflating was the stadium's setting. Originally parkland, the site had been laid out to host the 1924 Empire Exhibition, of which the stadium

Below: A visitors' map of the British Empire Exhibition, taken from the official guidebook. The Exhibition covered 87 hectares and was intended to showcase the best of industry, engineering and the arts from Britain and its 'Dominions and Colonies'.

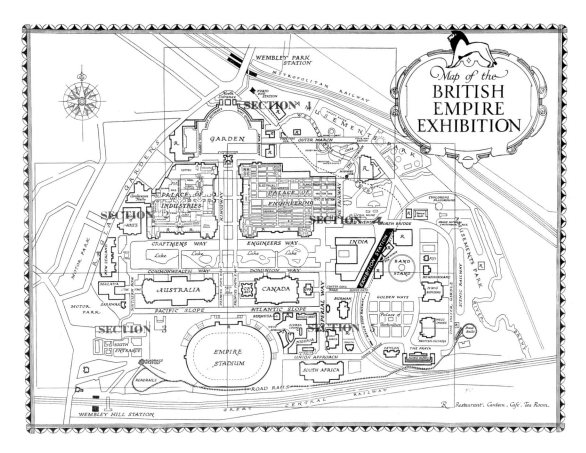

Far left: Her Majesty Queen Mary is shown around the British Empire Exhibition on the opening day, 23 April 1924.

Left: Looking towards the Palace of Engineering which was paired with the Palace of Industry.

Right: The largest concrete building in the world, covering six and a half times the area of Trafalgar Square, the Palace of Engineering displayed the wares and inventions of Britain's leading firms.

Wembley has arisen with its great pavilions as a shrine of Empire: it has become the natural meeting-place for the peoples of the British nations in every corner of the globe. *The Times*, 24 May 1924

Above: An aerial view of the British Empire Exhibition. The Empire Stadium, as it was known then, is seen with the Australian Pavilion, which was noted for eccentricities such as its display of scoured wool – a 16-foot ball sourced from every state and district in Australia.

formed the centrepiece. In 1934 the stadium was joined by the wonderful Empire Pool (now the Wembley Arena). But otherwise, as suburbia rose up on its borders throughout the 1930s, and the exhibition halls were demolished, destroying the integrity of the original masterplan, the stadium itself was left isolated. Compared with the grandeur surrounding Rome's Olympic Stadium, or the magisterial cohesion of Munich's Olympiapark and stadium, Wembley appeared unplanned and unloved.

But most damaging of all to Wembley's image were its inadequacies as a spectator venue. Neither the original architects, Sir John Simpson and Maxwell Ayrton, nor the engineer, Sir Owen Williams, had any experience of stadium design. Consequently, for all its innovative use of reinforced concrete, the building suffered a number of basic flaws, not least appalling viewing standards for up to a quarter of its 120,000 capacity, cramped concourses, and grossly inadequate toilet provision. Nor did successive remedial works ease these shortcomings. So the old Wembley Stadium was loved and hated, revered and reviled in almost equal measure.

No one doubted that it needed replacing. But with what, by whom, and how might this be achieved? In the end it took twelve years of planning, design and construction to unlock this conundrum, during which time Wembley's future fell subject to more detailed scrutiny than surely any other stadium in history. In the media Wembley became a national obsession, fuelled for the most part by commentators with pre-defined agendas and no real knowledge of large construction projects or stadium design. Consequently there are two quite separate, though parallel, narratives attached to the emergence of the new stadium.

The first, if recounted in full, would occupy a book twice the size of this one. Criticism of the project flew in from every angle and on almost every aspect – its cost, location, ownership and operation, contractual arrangements and funding. Arising from this, three parliamentary reports and two independent consultants' reports were commissioned. At least six major figures associated with the project from various public and private bodies either resigned or were ousted. It can also be argued that the careers of two government ministers suffered as a result of their interventions. (The English, it should be noted, have a tradition of denigrating major building projects, going back to St Paul's Cathedral, the Houses of Parliament and more recently the Millennium Dome. All three, of course, are now regarded as iconic structures.)

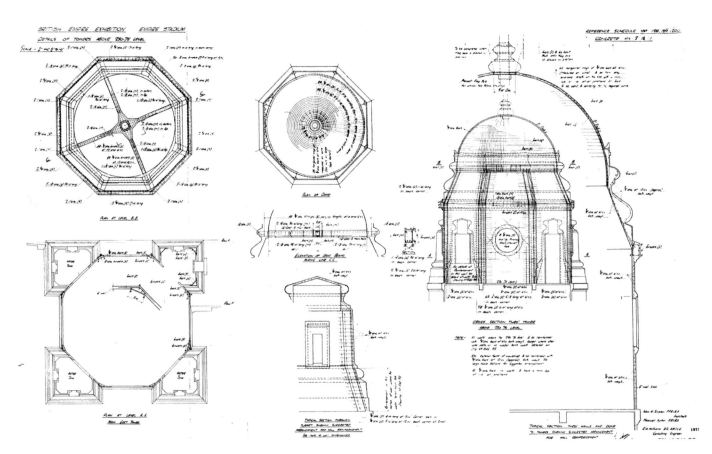

Above and right: Original construction drawings for Wembley Stadium's twin towers, whose design was influenced by Sir Edwin Lutyens' Viceroy's House in New Delhi. In common with all the buildings designed for the Empire Exhibition, the towers were constructed from reinforced concrete. The stadium itself required some 25,000 tonnes of concrete, but took just 300 days to complete. The towers' domes were engineered to very fine tolerances – their ferro-concrete shells being just 75mm deep.

The arch works not only structurally but also as an icon: it is an enormously successful London landmark and a worthy successor to the stage-set architecture of the old twin towers. Guide to the RIBA Awards, 2008

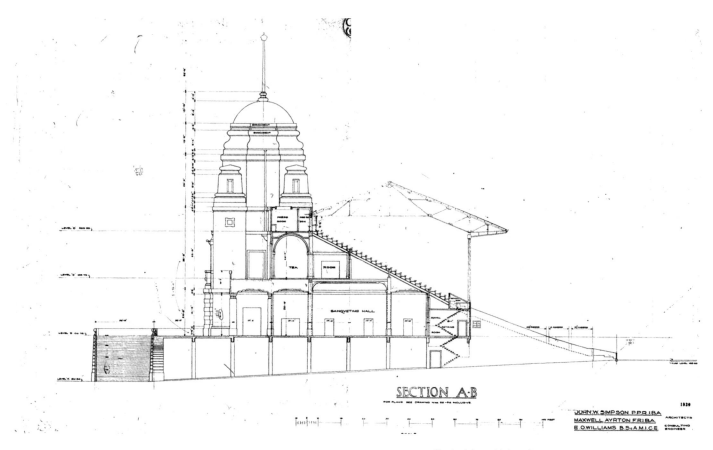

SECTION A·B

JOHN W. SIMPSON P.P.R.I.B.A
MAXWELL AYRTON F.R.I.B.A
E. O. WILLIAMS B.Sc.A.M.I.C.E.

Overleaf: An aerial view of Wembley in the late 1920s. As completed, the stadium accommodated 120,000 spectators, the great majority of them standing. Covered stands on the north and south sides of the stadium contained seats for 25,000.

Right: Fanny Blankers-Koen
of The Netherlands takes the
last flight of hurdles to win
the 80-metre race in a world
record time of 11.2 seconds
at the 1948 Olympics.

Left: Runners prepare to leave
the stadium at the start of
the 1948 Olympic marathon.

Above: Athletes parade around
Wembley Stadium during
the opening ceremony of the
Olympic Games, 29 July 1948.

Left: The cover of an Olympic Games special issue of *Picture Post*, August 1948.

Then there is a second possible narrative. Almost inevitably in the prevailing atmosphere of point-scoring, this aspect of the development received virtually no press coverage until the building was completed. But it is the one that concerns us here, and is the story of the new stadium's design. Not that this tale is any less complex.

Almost since its opening in 1923 architects and engineers had puzzled over strategies to improve Wembley Stadium. But as the building's fabric deteriorated, and as the commercial and social role of stadiums changed so radically from the 1970s onwards, these efforts took on a greater urgency. Two practices with stadium experience tried their hand in the early 1990s, the LOBB Partnership and Arup Associates.

Each incorporated into their speculative designs the stadium's twin towers, on the assumption that the Grade II listed structures were inviolable. Each assumed that the stadium and its surroundings – totalling some 70 acres – would remain in single ownership, if not necessarily in the hands of long-term owners Wembley plc.

However, neither scheme left the drawing board. The football industry had yet to gain the riches it would later accrue from television and sponsorship.

Equally, since the abolition of the Greater London Council in 1986, there existed within the capital no single administrative body that might coordinate a redevelopment strategy for Wembley. The local planning authority, Brent Borough Council, had certain powers but no access to funds.

Meanwhile, Wembley was about to find its role as the *de facto* national stadium under threat from provincial rivals. After failed Olympic bids by Birmingham (in 1986) and twice by Manchester (in 1990 and 1993), Britain's sporting bodies agreed that if, in future, a British city was going to bid for an Olympiad, it would be London.

For its part, Manchester decided to concentrate on securing the right to stage the Commonwealth Games in 2002. In the process of preparing that bid, Manchester not only secured public funding for an indoor arena, a velodrome and an aquatic centre, but its City Council argued that its proposed Commonwealth Games stadium should receive similar grant aid, and that, furthermore, it should become a replacement for Wembley.

Tired old Wembley, in leaderless London, thus had to face up to genuine competition for the first time in its history. But at least there was one possible source of funding to kick-start Wembley's renaissance –

Right: A poster for the 1948 Olympic Games. The hands of Big Ben point to four o'clock, the time at which the opening of the games was planned. The statue is Discobolus, the discus thrower from Ancient Greece.

the National Lottery, introduced in November 1994. Under the terms of the National Lottery Act, funds for sport-related projects are distributed via a government agency, Sport England, originally known as the Sports Council. However, its remit prevents the Council from inviting applications for Lottery grants from any one bidder. Nor could Wembley plc apply, as commercial entities are barred from the Lottery process.

Thus, in April 1995 the Sports Council found another means of starting the bidding, by holding an open competition for the creation of an 80,000-capacity 'national stadium' — one capable of staging three main sports: football, rugby league and athletics.

For stadium designers, the provision for athletics was by far the most problematic. Beyond Britain there are hundreds of stadiums featuring athletics tracks, with a pitch for football or rugby in the centre. However, none is popular with spectators of football or rugby. Viewing distances are extended and any sense of intimacy is lost.

Moreover, apart from the World Athletics Championships and the Olympics — events unlikely to be staged at any one venue more than once or twice in a fifty-year cycle, if at all — few athletics meetings attract significant attendances. For that reason, only publicly subsidised stadiums can justify the retention of a track. Certainly in Britain the combination of track and field has long been regarded as anathema, as a result of which there are no athletics stadiums in the country with a capacity greater than 25,000, and none of those is shared by senior football or rugby clubs.

Nevertheless, the Sports Council insisted that if the proposed Lottery grant of £120 million was to be forthcoming — the largest sum for any sports-related project to date — there had to be provision for athletics. It conceded, however, that the minimum capacity for an athletics event could be 65,000, rather than 80,000, to allow greater flexibility. (The Council based this calculation on the experience of the Stade de France in Paris, where the lower tier of seats retracts some 15 metres from football and rugby mode to reveal a track underneath. Although it was expensive, wasteful in terms of space, and resulted in compromised sightlines and viewing distances, the view was that if it could work for Paris then it could work for the new English national stadium.)

Shortly after the Sports Council's brief was announced, Huw Thomas of Foster + Parters called on Bob Heaver, Wembley Stadium's development director. Huw Thomas had been involved in the masterplanning of Manchester's Olympic bid, and argued that if Wembley was to have any success in outbidding

Left: Champions of the World! Bobby Moore holds the coveted Jules Rimet World Cup trophy aloft, 30 July 1966. England beat West Germany 4–2.

Manchester for Lottery funding as the national stadium, its management would have to prepare a cogent plan.

The Foster team drew up a masterplan that embraced the Wembley site as a whole. Its aim was to create a vast new public open space around the stadium that borrowed from the Centre Beaubourg and its piazza in Paris, and the National Gallery and Trafalgar Square in London. 'What was it', asked Huw Thomas, 'about Beaubourg, for example, that allowed a building with ostensibly no ground floor interface to interact with a public space? Similarly, we looked at the way the Campo in Siena transforms itself by populating the edge of its square with temporary structures. This led us to the idea of the stadium concourse being part of both the stadium itself and the public space.'

Within this masterplan the stadium shifted northwards to create space around its southern perimeter (itself bound by a railway cutting, too wide to bridge economically). To the north a range of sport, music and leisure outlets were linked to the stadium via an elliptically shaped piazza on two levels. Further commercial developments between this part of the site and the existing mixed-use developments opposite Wembley Park Underground station flanked Olympic Way, the main approach to the stadium. The idea

was to create a new urban complex, while also using commercial development to help fund the stadium's reconstruction.

Meanwhile, in addition to Wembley, four cities submitted proposals for the new national stadium: Birmingham, Bradford, Manchester and Sheffield. After three months of lobbying, in October 1995 the bids from Birmingham, Bradford and Sheffield were rejected by the Sports Council, leaving Wembley to fight it out with Manchester. Finally, in December 1996 Wembley was selected. In truth, of course, the ultimate decision rested less with the Sports Council or with any pro-London lobbyists and more with the Football Association. For the FA, the long Wembley tradition and the stadium's undoubted pulling power were powerful factors.

Wembley plc was now able to appoint its architects. Having established a strong working relationship with the practice, Foster + Partners was a clear favourite. But the practice had no stadium experience, and therefore opted to join forces with two other firms, HOK Sport and the LOBB Partnership.

Based in Kansas, HOK Sport (now known as Populous) are the world's most prolific stadium and arena designers. For their part the smaller London-based LOBB Partnership, led by Rod Sheard, had a

Right: Scottish fans invade the pitch and destroy the goalposts after beating England 2–1 in the British Home Championship match at Wembley, 4 June 1977.

Above: The audience at the Live Aid concert at Wembley Stadium – a 'global jukebox' of pop music that lasted sixteen hours – on 13 July 1985. Live Aid was seen on television around the world and raised millions of pounds to help relieve famine in Ethiopia.

The real skill in designing a stadium is not the technical stuff – it's designing a building that bottles emotion.
Norman Foster, 2012

solid track record in the UK. They were also working on Stadium Australia, venue for the 2000 Olympic Games in Sydney and on Cardiff's Millennium Stadium, Britain's first venue with a retractable roof. Huw Thomas recalls a meeting at Foster's Battersea studio to settle this tripartite agreement. 'After we had all declared our various expertise and renown, Norman said that if we were that good, why not call ourselves the World Stadium Team. The name stuck and we put in a bid as WST.'

The strategy worked: WST was appointed in May 1998. From Foster + Partners the team comprised Norman Foster, Ken Shuttleworth and Huw Thomas, with Alistair Lenczner (recruited from Arup, where he had worked on the Bari stadium), and Angus Campbell who, with Lenczner, would see the project through to completion. They would later be joined by Mouzhan Majidi, who led the project after completing Chek Lap Kok Airport in Hong Kong.

From HOK's office in Kansas City, David Manica was brought in to work on the design of the seating bowl, while from LOBB, in addition to Rod Sheard, Ben Vickery took a lead role. Appointed at the same time were structural engineers Mott MacDonald and Connell Wagner, and Stephen Morley from Modus Consulting Engineers, who had worked with LOBB on several

UK stadiums. However, while all seemed settled on the design front, in the corridors of power there were mighty stirrings. Because Lottery funds could not be given to Wembley plc (a commercial entity), a non-profit body called the English National Stadium Trust had been established to oversee the design and construction of the stadium. The plan was for the Trust to hire Wembley plc to manage the stadium on its behalf on a twenty-year lease. But as the Trust struggled to find an acceptable mechanism for this arrangement, only weeks after WST's appointment, in July 1998 an extraordinary turn of events transformed the situation. The FA, driven by one of the highest-profile figures in English football, the then Chelsea chairman Ken Bates, announced its intention to buy the stadium outright.

Bates' reasoning was that since football was providing most of the events it should take the lion's share of the profits. (It should be noted that the FA's previous deals with Wembley plc had been absurdly weighted in Wembley's favour.) The FA formed a subsidiary, Wembley National Stadium Limited (WNSL), to build and run the new stadium, with the English National Stadium Trust being given a place on WNSL's board to safeguard the public interest. It was a remarkable and quite unexpected coup.

With Wembley Stadium firmly in football's hands – purchased for £106 million in March 1999 – Bates drove forward his vision of how a modern stadium should be planned and financed. At his own stadium at Stamford Bridge, Bates had masterminded the creation of an entirely novel form of development. Called Chelsea Village, this placed the stadium at the centre of a commercial hub that incorporated a hotel, restaurants, a health club, visitor attraction and banqueting suites – a facility that could be used 365 days a year, rather than simply on match days. Bates sought to repeat this formula at Wembley, expanding the stadium brief to include a 2,000-seat restaurant, a hotel and office space – in effect, a 'Wembley Village'.

Joined by a new WNSL chief executive, Bob Stubbs – who had first acted as a consultant to the Sports Council on the National Stadium project – Bates now dominated proceedings, with meetings held not at Wembley but at Chelsea. Norman Foster quickly grew to respect Bates' no-nonsense approach, his capacity to absorb detail and his determination to make things happen in the face of all manner of obstacles. Bates also shared Foster's vision for a stadium that connected practically and economically with the surrounding urban infrastructure.

Once asked to nominate his favourite building, Norman Foster selected a Boeing 747. In one important respect, a modern stadium provides a similar business model. Although designed to hold the maximum number of economy passengers, the aircraft's economic viability depends on revenues from the passengers flying in business and first class. Reflecting this approach, Bates and Stubbs determined that Wembley would hold 90,000 seats, rather than 80,000, but of those, the entire middle tier (eventually consisting of 16,000 seats) would be devoted to executive boxes and club seats. In this way, roughly two thirds of ticketing revenue would be earned from one fifth of the total capacity. (The 747 analogy would later be extended to the stadium toilets, whose numbers are provided in the same, if not a higher ratio than on a passenger jet.)

A further key design issue concerned the retention or otherwise of the stadium's iconic twin towers.

The original stadium had been designed for 100,000 spectators, the majority of whom stood on terracing. Conversion to an all-seated configuration in 1990 resulted in a drop in capacity to 80,000, but depended on extremely narrow seat tread depths of 640mm, and below average seat widths of 410mm. By the early 1990s the standard was for tread depths

Left: The Nelson Mandela concert at Wembley Stadium, 16 April 1990. Over a billion people across five continents watched on television as Mandela himself took the stage.

Left: Balloons are released at Wembley signalling the start of Euro '96, 8 June 1996. England drew 1–1 with Switzerland in the opening game.

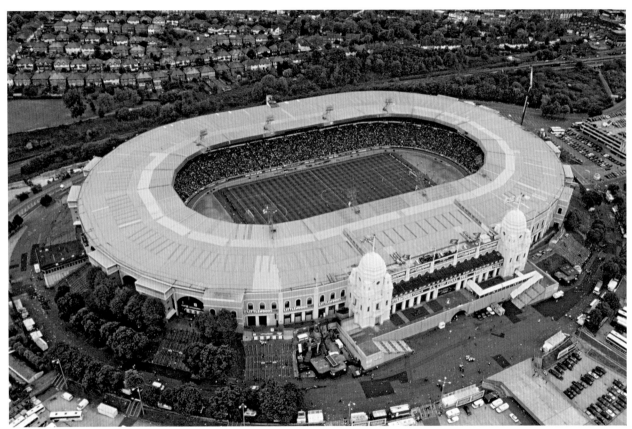

Above: An aerial view of Wembley Stadium towards the end of its active life. Although by 1963 it was entirely roofed, and by 1990 had become an all-seat venue, with a maximum capacity of 78,000, the facilities it provided were poor.

of 760mm and seat widths of 500mm. For Wembley, based on the experience of Stadium Australia, the design team opted for still more generous dimensions of 800mm and 500mm respectively, thereby allowing each spectator 30 per cent more room than in the old stadium.

Crucially, this decision extended the new stadium's footprint considerably – to 300 metres east to west and 280 metres north to south – on what was already a confined site. As there was no room on the southern flank of the site (bound as it is by the railway cutting), that meant expansion could only take place on the northern side; but that was where the towers stood.

Throughout 1999 speculation mounted as to the towers' fate. As Grade II listed structures, demolition required consent from English Heritage. But what if the towers could be moved and incorporated within the new design? Rallying to the cause, one engineer proposed sliding the towers on platforms to another part of the site. Another option was to jack the domes on to steel frames so that they might be incorporated into the new stadium structure (which would otherwise dwarf the towers at their original height).

Significantly, English Heritage agreed with the design team that the presence of the towers, overpowered by the scale of the new stadium, would be an unnecessarily inhibiting factor. That said, it was incumbent on the team to come up with a similarly iconic feature to take the towers' place.

Another crucial factor was the provision of an athletics track. Studies by LOBB concluded that the design solution adopted at the Stade de France, using retractable seating, wasted space and offered few benefits for spectators in either athletics or football mode. Instead, Rod Sheard suggested that if and when Wembley was ever to stage an athletics event, a temporary platform could be built over the pitch and the first few rows of seating, and an athletics track laid on top of it. Originally it was thought that this platform would need precast concrete supports, but in time the team came to favour a more lightweight and cost-effective steel solution.

Whichever modular system might eventually emerge, the geometry would be the same. A temporary platform would allow the front row of lower tier seats, in football and rugby mode, to be placed within a more intimate range of 9-17 metres from the touchlines, compared with a range of 11-29 metres at Stade de France. Moreover, although a temporary platform would reduce the stadium's seating capacity from 90,000 in football mode to around 68,400 in athletics mode, this was still above the 65,000 limit required by the brief.

This solution should have been welcomed. It was simple, low-tech, and took consideration of the fact that there might well be only one or two occasions in the building's entire life when such a platform would be needed. Yet the response from government and the athletics lobby could hardly have been more hostile. Ken Bates was accused of hijacking the stadium project for football's benefit (to which he responded that football was raising all the capital and providing all the guarantees). It was also claimed that Wembley would never be able to host an Olympics using the platform solution, because the minimum capacity demanded by the International Olympic Committee was not 65,000 but 75,000. For weeks these figures were contested (even among IOC members), but the original terms of the brief – in which no mention of Olympic capability had been mentioned – were a matter of record. (Interestingly, the IOC report on the 2012 Olympic requirements states that the minimum capacity requirement for athletics and ceremonies in the stadium is 60,000.)

Opponents of the platform scheme also tried to prove, without success, that sightlines for athletics at Wembley would be inferior to those for athletics at the Stade de France. Suddenly everyone was an expert, among them the newly appointed sports minister,

Kate Hoey, whose first pronouncement was that, given the option, she would happily cancel the Wembley project altogether.

As the furore continued in the press, the first plans for the new stadium were unveiled at Wembley on 29 July 1999. But it was the stadium's costs and the athletics issue which seemed to occupy most attention on the day. The design was barely commented on at all. Perhaps this was just as well, because even as the scheme was being unveiled, Norman Foster was harbouring second thoughts about a key element.

This concerned the support system for the stadium roof. A requirement of the brief was that the pitch had to consist of natural turf, rather than synthetic fibres (as has become common in North America), and that every effort should be made to guarantee the turf as much light and ventilation as possible so that pitch quality would not suffer as it has done at so many large modern stadiums with high-profile stands.

In order to achieve this, the design team came up with a system whereby sections of the roof over the south, east and west of the three-tier seating bowl are retractable, the moveable sections covering spectator areas only, not the entire pitch. To bear the load of the fixed northern side of the roof, the designers proposed

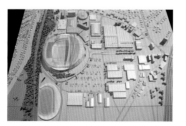

Left: A model of the stadium, including provision for an athletics warm-up track to the east of the arena, seen lower left in this image.

Our masterplan was concerned with establishing a relationship between the stadium and a new public space. Conceptually, the reference points were the Centre Pompidou and its piazza and the National Gallery and Trafalgar Square. Huw Thomas, Foster + Partners, 2012

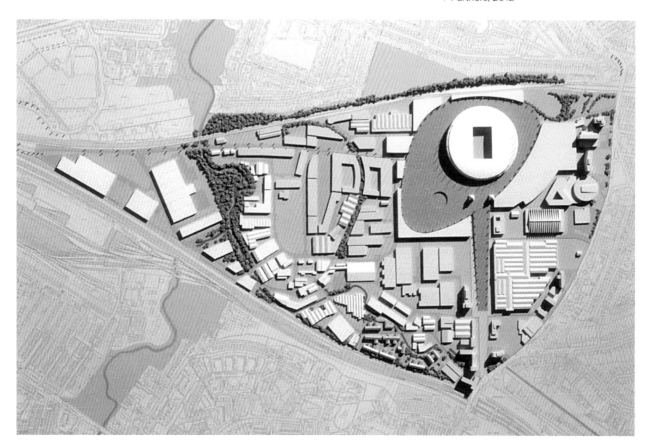

Above: The first masterplanning model of the stadium and its surroundings, dating from 1996. The stadium forms the focus of a new public urban space.

The first thing we asked was 'how can we create a new generation stadium and what form does that take?' Any proposal had to be conceptually robust enough to withstand many challenges – financial and political.
Norman Foster, 2012

Above: A new Wembley Stadium, as first envisaged by the Foster team in 1995. This early scheme had a principal approach from the north, with new facilities accommodated on land to be acquired behind the old stadium. This would have required a significantly larger site than was ultimately available.

erecting four 130-metre-high steel masts in front of the stadium's main facade, from which supporting cables would be suspended.

On the day of the unveiling very little was said about these masts, other than a comment by the England manager Kevin Keegan that they reminded him of the Stade de France. But within the design team there were almost immediate misgivings. Norman Foster recalled, 'My worry was that the mast structure was not in any way special to Wembley and in fact had a lot of associations with other building types – the circus tent, for example'. Mouzhan Majidi remembers, 'Norman was worried that the masts did not present a strong enough *image*. As a team we also had doubts about them from a structural standpoint. So it was that just a couple of days after the unveiling we were all sitting down trying to redesign it.'

That weekend found Foster cycling near Bayreuth, where he had been attending the annual festival, and it was in the German countryside that the idea of a 'super arch' struck him. A rapid exchange of faxes ensued between Foster and Alistair Lenczner, a structural engineer based in the Foster studio in London; Foster sending sketches, Lenczner working out how such a structure could be constructed and located on the tight site. It quickly emerged that the

determining structural factor would be the height of the arch, and that this height would have to rise so high above the London skyline that Wembley would gain an unparalleled visibility.

Recalling those hectic few days, Lenczner says, 'Immediately we were convinced that the arch was the way to go – that it could replace the twin towers with an incredibly powerful iconic image. We were also confident that the engineers would agree that the arch was a better solution.'

First thing on the Monday morning Mouzhan Majidi briefed the Foster model shop to make a rudimentary model of the arch proposal, and as soon as it was ready it was taken to Rod Sheard at HOK Sport's offices. 'To his great credit,' Lenczner recalls, 'Rod wasn't upset that we were having second thoughts and immediately supported the new design.'

'The next step', Lenczner says, 'was for Norman to present it to the FA, or rather to Ken Bates. So he took a stack of sketches and walked over the river to Chelsea Village. Ken had no idea what the meeting was about and so had said to Norman, "Let's meet in the pub". And it was there that Norman took him through the reasoning behind the change. And again, like every other member of the team, Ken Bates went for the new version, and made the really big decision to

change the design.' That one decision was to transform the public's perception of the project. Not only did the arch suppress any lingering regrets about the loss of the twin towers, it also provided the new stadium with a powerful and instantly recognisable motif.

Statistics relating to the arch's construction have become part of the Wembley narrative. Its span of 315 metres is larger than any other arch in the world. It towers 133 metres above the pitch, almost as tall as the London Eye (the capital's favourite new icon). A double-decker bus or train could pass through its core. Best of all, it offers a vital focal counterpoint to the mass of the stadium bowl. And as Alistair Lenczner emphasises, the arch uses only 1,750 tonnes of steel, making it lighter and thus more economical than the mast solution.

It is a measure of how many other distractions there were at the time that hardly a single press report voiced any comment on this sudden change of plan. Instead, the press continued to concentrate on the sports minister's barrage of comments about the athletics track.

WNSL's 1,600-page planning application was submitted to Brent Council in November 1999. But the press continued to present the Wembley scheme as if it was doomed to failure. One could only hope that the architects were issued with copies of Rudyard Kipling's poem 'If', with its exhortation, 'If you can keep your head when all about you are losing theirs …'

Planning approval for the revised scheme came through in June 2000. But that was by no means the end of Wembley's 'woes'. As plans were drawn up for the old stadium's final curtain call – an England versus Germany friendly – press reports said that the scheme's costs had risen to £600 million: almost twice the amount stated a year earlier. In fact, the additional costs – which included the £106 million purchase of the site and legal, professional and administrative fees – were independent of the stadium construction costs, which had been fixed at a guaranteed maximum price of £326.5 million by the contractors Multiplex (the giant Australian firm that had built Stadium Australia).

Even with later revisions, which took the total stadium cost to £352 million, the average of £3,900 per seat is still comparable with other major stadium developments in North America, Japan and Europe. But the press had no time for such distinctions. The story was that costs were spiralling and the stadium had to be part of the problem.

Old Wembley's final match turned out to be a dreadful letdown. Played in pouring rain on a grey

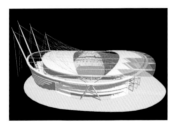

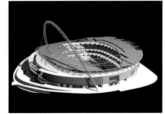

JULY 1999

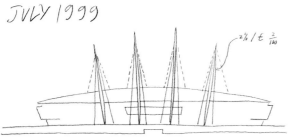

$2\% / E \frac{3}{100}$

The image - The barriers - fortress Wembley
Well tried - also tents
- Domes

OUTSIDE

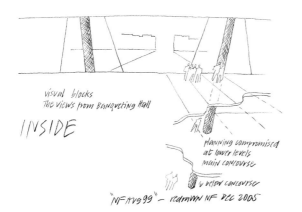

visual blocks
The views from Banqueting Hall

INSIDE

planning compromised
at lower levels
main concourse

4 below concourse

"NF AVG 99" - redrawn NF DEC 2005

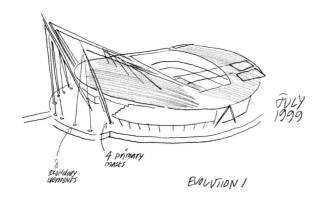

8 secondary elements

4 primary masts

JULY 1999

EVOLUTION !

AUGUST 1999

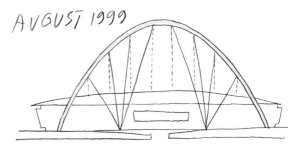

The Arch - triumphant
inviting - gateway - permanent
emblematic symbol

OUTSIDE

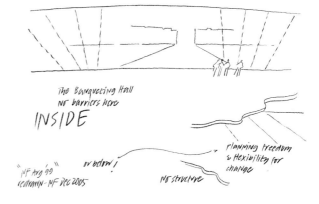

The Banqueting Hall
no barriers here

INSIDE

"NF Aug 99"
redrawn - NF DEC 2005

or below !

no structure

planning freedom
& flexibility for
change

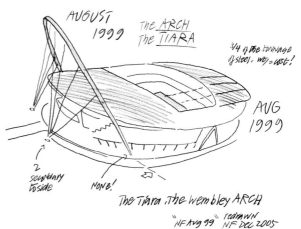

AUGUST 1999 The ARCH The TIARA

¾ of the tonnage
of steel, why = cost !

AUG 1999

2 secondary outside

NONE !

The Tiara . The Wembley ARCH

"NF Aug 99" redrawn
NF Dec 2005

October afternoon, an uninspired England were beaten 1–0, after which the crestfallen manager, Kevin Keegan, resigned.

Three months later there followed another high profile resignation. After the proposed hotel and office developments were dropped from the scheme and under increasing pressure from his counterparts at the FA, in December 2000 Ken Bates stood down from the chairmanship of WNSL. 'Even Jesus Christ suffered only one Pontius Pilate,' remarked the ever-caustic Bates: 'I had a whole team of them.'

Critics began to call for a scaled down project. There was even talk of Birmingham re-entering the fray. However, after detailed scrutiny of the costs, Bates' replacement at WNSL, Sir Rodney Walker, announced in early 2001 that he saw no need to amend the plans further. Bates had been vindicated. The design stood; but it also remained on the drawing board. While WNSL's bankers, the German bank WestLB, sought to arrange the loan of £433 million needed to trigger the reconstruction, the old stadium remained boarded up and empty for two years: time aplenty for the press to maintain its barrage of negative reporting, time for a new chief executive to be installed at WNSL, and in government for the appointment of a new culture secretary.

Left: An early visualisation of the arch. Consisting of steel rings connected by spiralling tubular chords, the arch tapers at each end and rests on concrete bases, founded on piles 35 metres deep. Inclined 68 degrees to the vertical, the arch is secured by cables tied to the main stadium structure.

Left: The arch scheme is presented to the FA and FIFA as part of England's bid for the 2006 World Cup. From left: Ken Bates, England football team manager Kevin Keegan and Norman Foster.

Back at Wembley, meanwhile, hope of a coherent masterplan for the site faded when, in August 2002, 41 acres of the adjoining site, containing the Wembley Exhibition Centre, the Wembley Arena, various car parks and access routes, were sold by a beleaguered Wembley plc to a development company, Quintain Estates, plus a further 11 acres comprising the two last plots of the 1924 Empire Exhibition site. Thus ownership of the Wembley site was divided for the first time since 1923.

Finally, in late 2002, once the finance agreements had been signed, demolition of the old stadium commenced. However, it would take another five years before the new stadium was ready. Predictably, throughout this period scare stories concerning the construction gathered their own momentum. As was widely reported, Multiplex suffered financial losses in the process. There were disputes with subcontractors, problems with unions. Yet another chief executive at WNSL was appointed, as was a new chairman and another new chief executive at the FA. In February 2004 a third House of Commons report was published. Had the carpets been in place by this stage, they would surely have been soaked in blood.

And all the while the stadium bowl rose up on the horizon, step by step, until in June 2004, as the arch

began its ascent on the skyline, suddenly, but quite perceptibly, a change in the public mood could be discerned. The final remaining executive box leases were sold. Nearly all the 15,000 club seats were sold. At one point the box office was taking receipts of £1 million a day. Here, clearly, was no ordinary stadium. Here was a colossus – it only needed some physical manifestation of the design to have the public come flocking to its gates.

The world is full of anonymous stadiums that few people recognise but that function perfectly adequately. Equally there are numerous examples of eye-catching stadiums that are beloved by architectural critics, yet loathed by spectators. Considering how successful the Romans were in solving most of the geometric and structural issues inherent in the type – as evidenced by the Colosseum – it is remarkable how frequently twentieth-century architects managed to sacrifice function for form. Tony Garnier at the Stade de Gerland, Lyon (1920), Pier Luigi Nervi at the Stadio Comunale, Florence (1932), Frei Otto's undulating acrylic, tent-like canopy at the Olympiastadion, Munich (1972); each was acclaimed by the critics, yet remained flawed as a mass-spectator facility.

Where Foster and the World Stadium Team parted from this trend was in their determination to ensure

Right: Norman Foster, Ken Bates and FIFA representatives discuss the scheme.

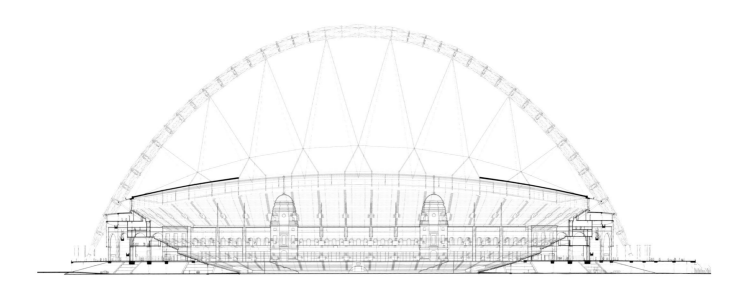

Above: An east-west section
through the new stadium
compared with an elevation of
the old. Standing 133 metres
high, spanning 315 metres and
weighing 1,750 tonnes, the arch
is almost four times taller than
the original twin towers.

Right: A plan of the new Wembley
compared with the old. Twice the
size of its predecessor, the new
stadium is among the most
spacious in the world. Every one
of the 90,000 seats has clear
sightlines, a marked contrast with
the 20 to 25 per cent of seats
whose views were obscured
by pillars in the old stadium.

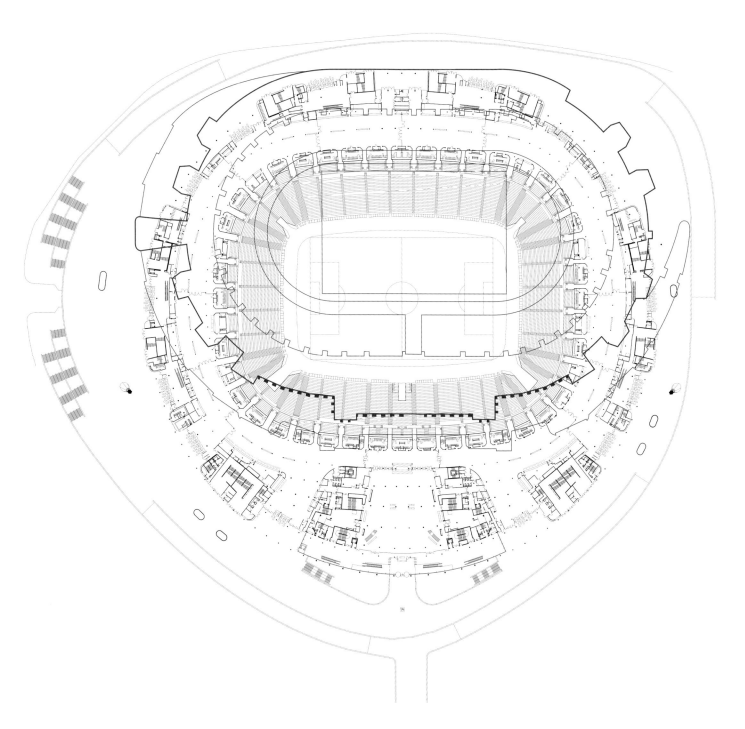

the pure functionality of the design. From the pitch outwards, there are no features that do not contribute to the stadium's ability to accommodate a full house, in maximum comfort, and with maximum visibility.

At the centre of this design matrix lies the pitch, 4 metres below the level of the old Wembley turf and layered on a substructure of sand and soil, interlaced with piped systems for drainage, ventilation and under-soil heating. These systems allow air to circulate to promote root growth, and for warm water pipes to provide protection against frost.

To allow the maximum amount of daylight to fall on the pitch, moveable panels in the roof can be adjusted to meet varying conditions. As photographs taken after the stadium's completion confirmed, the predictions on which these designs were based turned out to be almost 100 per cent accurate. At 3.00pm on a May afternoon (the traditional date for the Cup Final), the variation in shade recorded turned out to be within half a metre of the computerised model.

However, no computer model was able to predict the exceptionally wet summer that coincided with Wembley's completion. That, combined with the effects of an American gridiron football match, tested the new pitch systems to the full during Wembley's first months and refinements have since proved necessary. But

most stadium pitches take several years to bed down and mature, and in that sense, the insistence on a natural turf pitch for Wembley will always require extra vigilance and care.

Of course, nowadays a stadium pitch is not only for sport, but for accommodating concert audiences. At Wembley there is provision for up to 20,000 people to stand on the pitch, not on the turf but on a protective system of moulded and interlocking panels, which can remain in place for several days without damaging the grass. Wembley's in-house sound system can be similarly geared towards those on the pitch, as well as those in the stands.

Around the pitch stands the six-storey 'drum', consisting of seating tiers on the inner rim, and concourses and hospitality areas on the outer. At basement level a service road provides 360-degree vehicle access (for television and concert trucks as well as service vehicles). This road also provides a secure point of entry for players, performers, officials and VIPs. Once again, the statistics for these 'back-of-house' areas have been repeatedly cited. But the fact that there are more than 2,600 lavatories – more than any other stadium in the world – becomes more meaningful when one considers that this is six times more than the old stadium.

Right: The giant German excavator 'Goliath' clears the site; the twin towers remain in the background – the last pieces to go. The towers were finally demolished on 7 February 2003.

Far left: Erection of the arch begins, steel diagrid sections of the arch having been assembled on the pitch.

Left: Temporarily vertical, the arch reaches its apex; five temporary stays anchor the arch while hefty concrete cores (visible in the foreground) prevent its release.

Above: An aerial view of the stadium under construction; the roof structure below the arch is assembled and the seating bowl completed.

Similarly, that there are restaurant facilities for up to 15,000 diners at a single sitting (or one in six of the 90,000 capacity) has to be seen in the context of the capital's already vast corporate hospitality market. Wembley, as Ken Bates hoped it would, has London's largest single banqueting room, holding 2,000 guests. This room, and three of its other restaurants, are indeed the city's four largest.

But what of the seating bowl itself? Given the number of elliptically shaped stadiums in the world it might be imagined that few variations in design are possible. Yet the possibilities are infinite, with each bowl exhibiting a subtle interplay of aisles, gangways, vomitories and barriers. At Wembley, the architects had no choice over the colour of the tip-up seats. These had to be the same red as used in the old stadium. But look closely and you see that the design team took great care with spacing each row of seats to avoid the awkward gaps that so often appear in the corners of stadiums. This seamless quality adds greatly to the uniformity of the bowl, and therefore to the visual impact of the three concentric levels. Of these, the lowest tier seats 34,303; the centre tier, including club seats and 160 hospitality suites and the Royal Box, accommodates 16,532; while the upper tier seats 39,165.

Above: The 133-metre-high Wembley arch compared with other London landmarks: 30 St Mary Axe, the London Eye, the BT Tower, Big Ben and Nelson's Column.

Stadium designers frequently debate the relative merits of having small lower tiers and larger upper tiers, or vice versa. Here the equilibrium between the two and the absence of a large overhang over the central tier means that the bowl has a unity that is rare in stadiums of more than 50,000 capacity. Crucially – because at a stadium the crowd is as much a part of the spectacle as the performers – this allows spectators in almost every part of the stadium to see from their seat as much of the other spectator accommodation as is possible.

This geometry does mean, however, that instead of winning captains having to climb just thirty-nine steps to receive their cup and medals from the Royal Box, as in the old stadium, they must now face 107 steps. But again, this was part of the design brief. The presentation of honours from a centrally placed Royal Box was part of the old Wembley's appeal, whereas at other modern stadiums the ceremony is usually performed on platforms placed on the pitch. Not the Wembley way at all.

But the ultimate test for any new stadium is how the spectator responds to it as a building. Often commentators use the expression 'wow factor'. By this they mean a stadium's ability to excite and inspire, and also its visual identity. Put bluntly, what can it

offer that another stadium cannot? Because of its history and the events staged there, Wembley has a cachet that other stadiums cannot match. But what the old stadium never had was comfort or amenity levels commensurate with its status, a situation that has changed completely.

That the new stadium stands resplendent on the north-west London skyline, its arch a towering statement of engineering finesse; that its amenities have been praised by both spectators and athletes; that its high standards of materials and finishes far outstrip popular expectations, confirms what all its backers argued from the beginning. That design excellence must override all other considerations, and that, bluntly, the end will justify the means. But what a struggle it was.

Wembley's turnstiles opened for its first trial match, an England Under 21 friendly against Italy, on 24 March 2007. The first full house of 90,000 spectators, for the FA Cup Final between Manchester United and Chelsea, followed on 19 May.

Alas for John Roberts, the chairman of Multiplex, the opening came too late. The man described by Norman Foster as one of the two key individuals in bringing the project to fruition died a year earlier. The other, Ken Bates, had in the meantime moved on to become chairman of another football club, Leeds United.

Wembley, it might be argued, is a true creation of the twenty-first century. Wired for sound and light, plugged into the digital world, marketed as a brand and hired out for one use or another on almost every day of the year, its ultimate function is part live theatre and part television studio. Once the players of clubs like Manchester United and Chelsea take centre stage, the architects, engineers and the legions of contractors who pieced it together can only look on from the sidelines.

In the stadium's first three months it hosted six major football matches, one Rugby League Challenge Cup Final, seven pop music concerts (featuring such stars as George Michael, Elton John, Status Quo, Duran Duran, Genesis and Madonna) and a regular series of exhibitions and corporate events. It was even transformed as the venue for a mini-motor-racing tournament, with a temporary tarmac track laid above the pitch. When London was chosen as the host city for the XXX Olympiad in 2012, Wembley was the natural venue for the football finals; and should there ever be a need to stage an athletics event, the plans for a platform are ready and waiting to be implemented – all as planned.

Right: The 6-metre-high statue of Bobby Moore by sculptor Philip Jackson pays tribute to one of England's greatest footballers. Moore made 108 appearances for England and 642 appearances for West Ham.

Above: An aerial view of the newly completed stadium, seen from the north-west; the Wembley Arena is in the foreground.

Right: The stadium seen from the south-west; the roof is seen here in the open position.

Big buildings need big gestures, and just seeing the arch from a distance is enough to set your heart racing. Mark Hines, *The Architects' Journal*, 5 June 2008

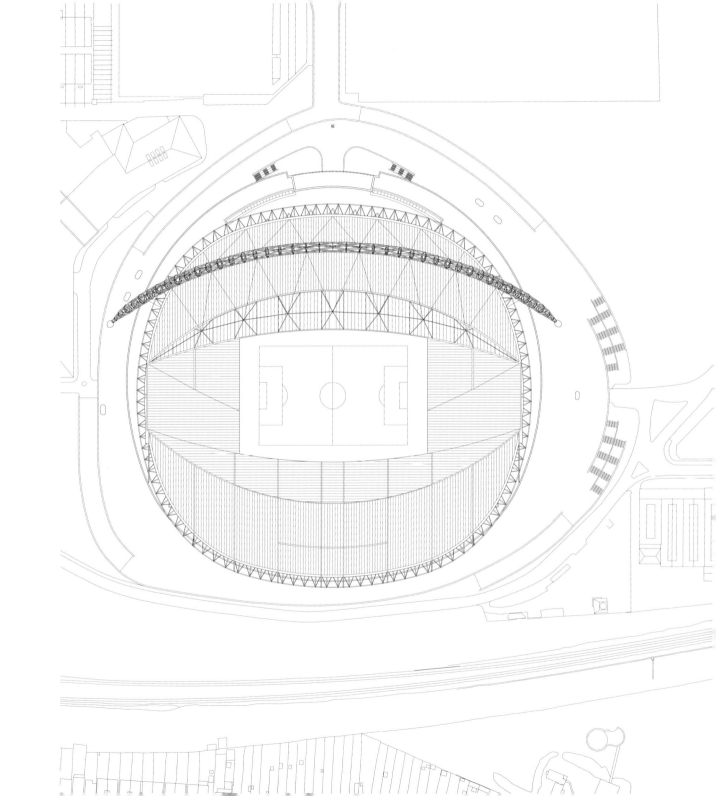

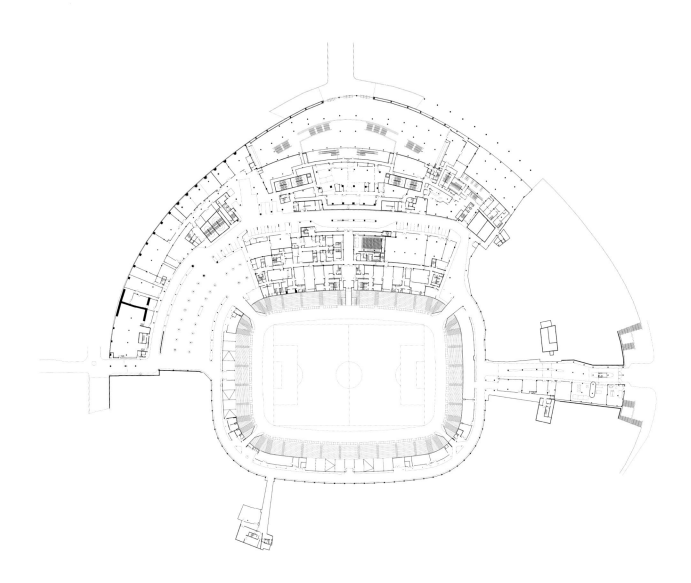

Left: Site plan, showing the
roof in the closed position.

Above: Plan at Level B2,
corresponding with the pitch.

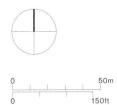

0   50m

0   150ft

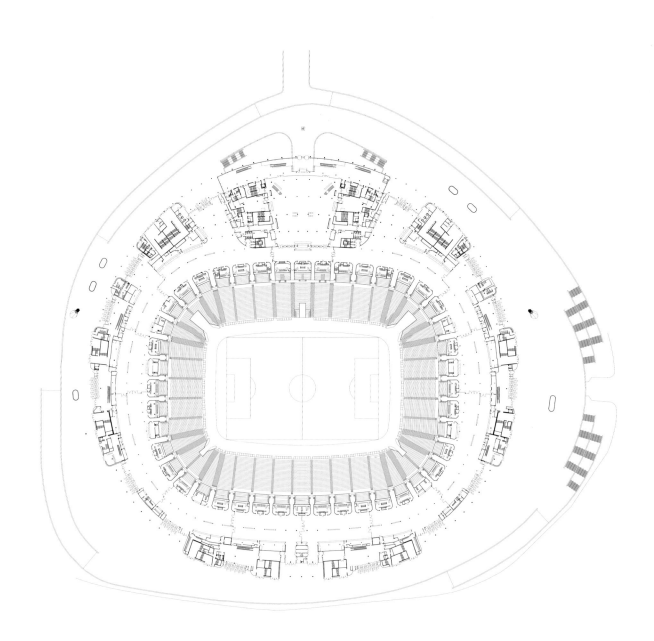

0   50m

0   150ft

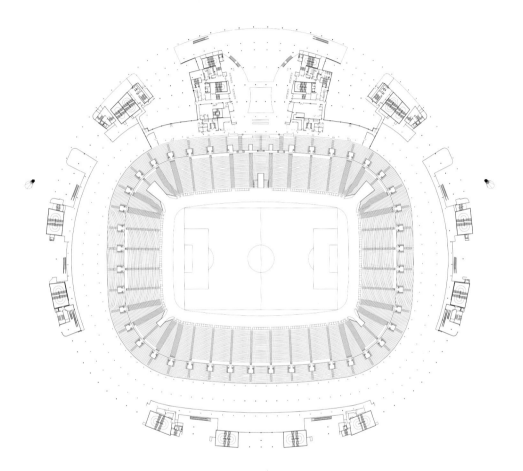

Left: Plan at Level 00, the
lower public concourse.

Above: Plan at Level 02, the
Club Wembley concourse.

Overleaf: The stadium
approached from the west.

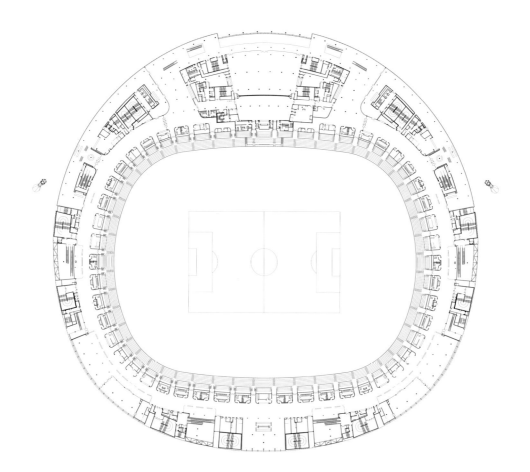

Above: Plan at Level 03, which
provides hospitality boxes.

Right: Plan at Level 04, which
provides hospitality boxes and
WNSL offices.

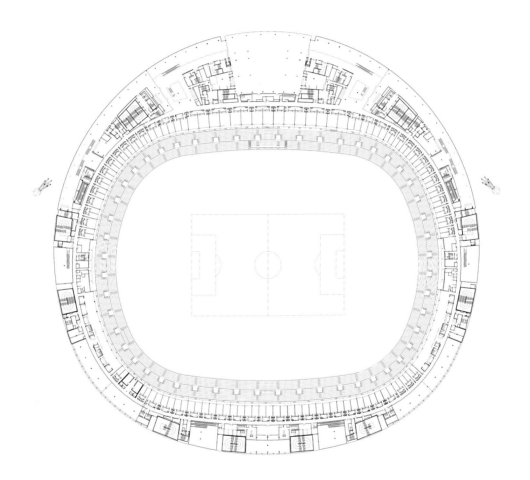

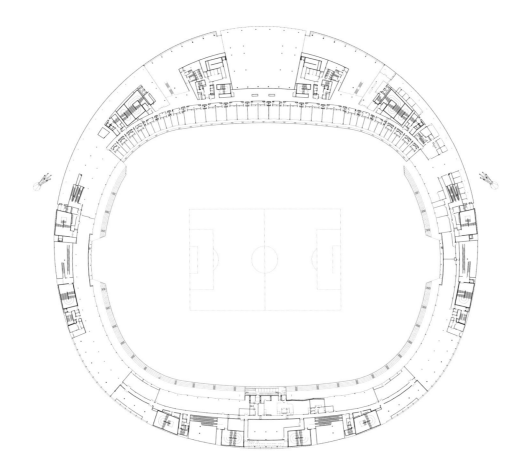

Above: Plan at Level 05,
the upper concourse.

Right: Plan at Level 06, the
highest seating tier, showing
the full seating bowl.

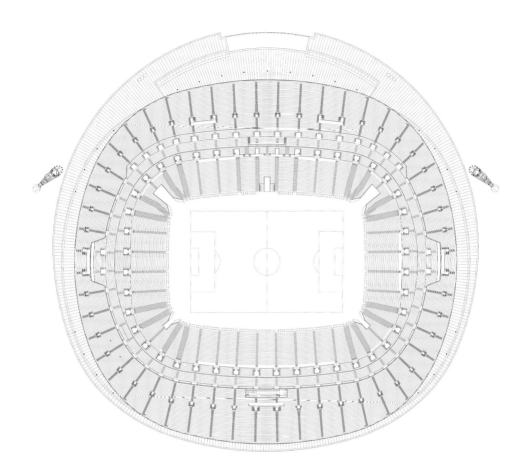

Left: Framed by the Wembley arch, fans and rivals bring Olympic Way alive with colour.

Above: Broad and spacious, the lower concourse circulation for general admission easily accommodates a thronging football crowd.

Left: One of several public cafés that together cater for 10,500 seated meals at every event.

Above: Hospitality areas flank the northern side of the pitch and open on to the individual boxes.

Left and above: The atrium on the north side provides vertical circulation to the hospitality areas and acts as a pre-function gathering space. Escalators – rare in British stadiums – take fans to the upper tiers.

Overleaf: An east-west cross-section, looking north towards the arch.

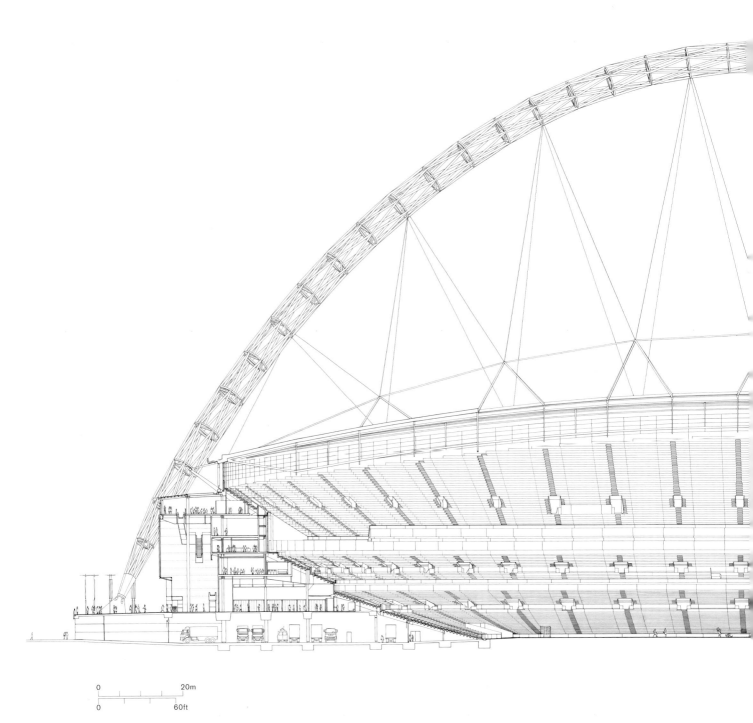

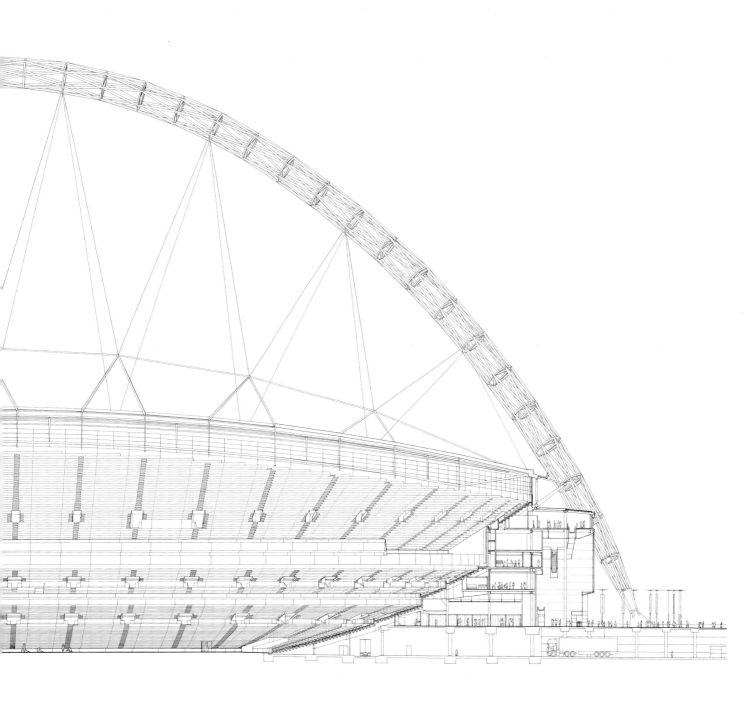

Previous pages: A near-capacity crowd in the stadium for the England versus Czech Republic international, 8 August 2008. England and Czech Republic drew 2–2.

Left: The English and Brazilian teams file out of the tunnel for the first full international in the new stadium, 1 June 2007. England and Brazil drew 1–1.

Above: The England flag is spread out on the pitch before the kick-off.

The new Wembley Stadium bowl is a truly magnificent space. To emerge through one of its vomitories on a match day is to experience spatial 'compression and release' at an ultimate level. One must marvel at just how effortless it all seems.
Neven Sidor, *Architecture Today*, May 2007

Above: A full stadium for the
Liverpool versus Everton FA
Cup semi-final, 14 April 2012.
Liverpool beat Everton 2 –1.

Overleaf: A north-south
cross-section through the
stadium bowl. The seating bowl
comprises three main tiers, with
a total capacity of 90,000.

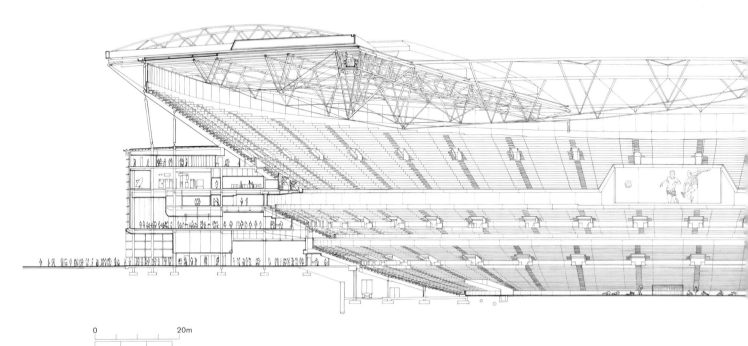

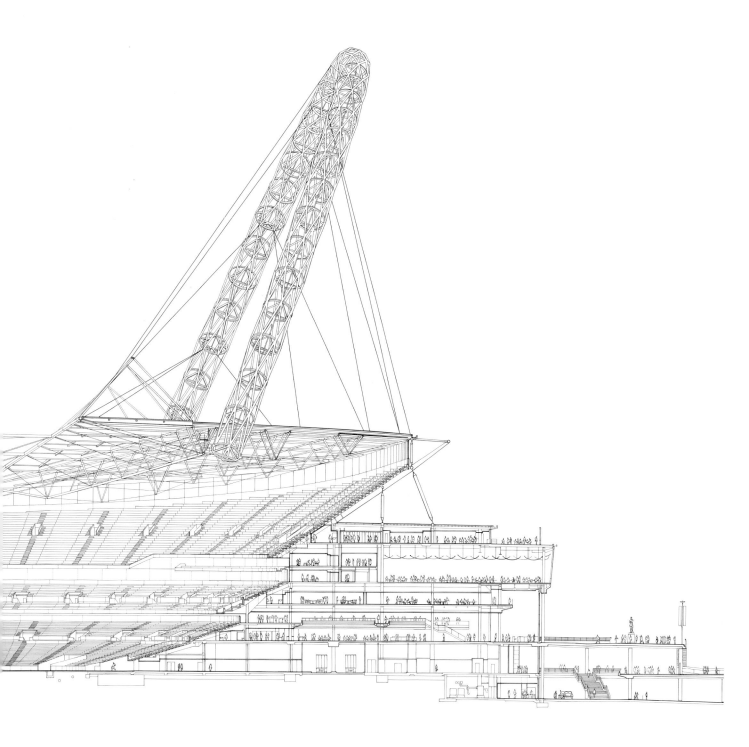

Wembley's sheer scale is stunning – the entire old stadium would fit inside the perimeter. Yet there is still a certain intimacy to the place.
Rob Shepherd, *News of the World*, 20 May 2007

Left: Manchester United fans re-ignite the famous 'Wembley roar' in the new stadium.

Above: A fitting opening for Wembley. The Red Arrows soar overhead before kick-off for the 2007 FA Cup Final, Chelsea versus Manchester United, 19 May 2007.

Above: The Race of Champions is an annual international motor sport event that brings together the world's finest drivers from all the competition disciplines – on four wheels and two – and allows them to battle head-to-head in identical cars. The twentieth Race of Champions was staged at Wembley on 16 December 2007.

Right: A heat of the Race of Champions; the final was won by the Swedish DTM Audi driver, Mattias Ekström who beat seven-time Formula One champion, Michael Schumacher.

Overleaf: Seen illuminated in anticipation of an evening match, the stadium bowl is viewed from one of the hospitality boxes on Level 03.

Above: The England team warms up on the Wembley pitch prior to the international friendly against Ghana, 29 March 2011; England drew 1–1. The huge contingent of Ghanaian fans helped to create a memorable atmosphere.

Right: Wembley Stadium, seen from Olympic Way, illuminated for an evening match.

Overleaf: Muse make their
Wembley Stadium debut,
16 June 2007. A temporary
platform is erected above the
pitch for concerts, bringing fans
as close as possible to the stage.

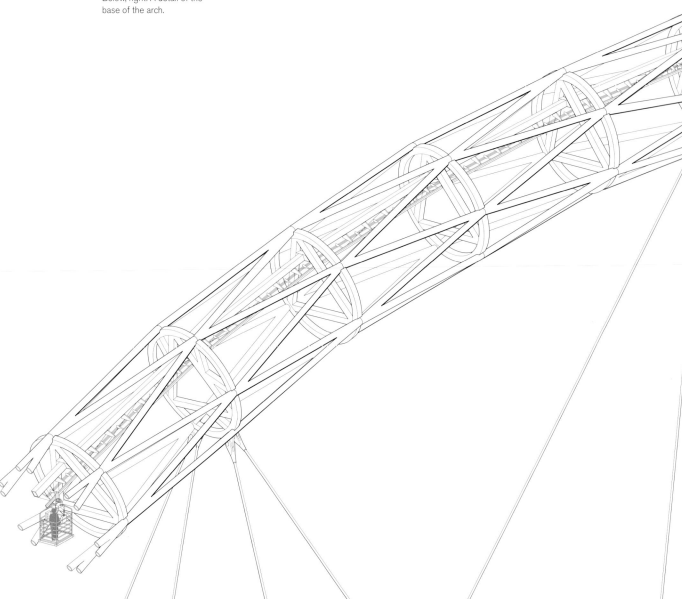

Below: A segment of the arch, with suspension cables attached; the arch has a span of 315 metres, is 133 metres high and weighs 1,750 tonnes.

Below, right: A detail of the base of the arch.

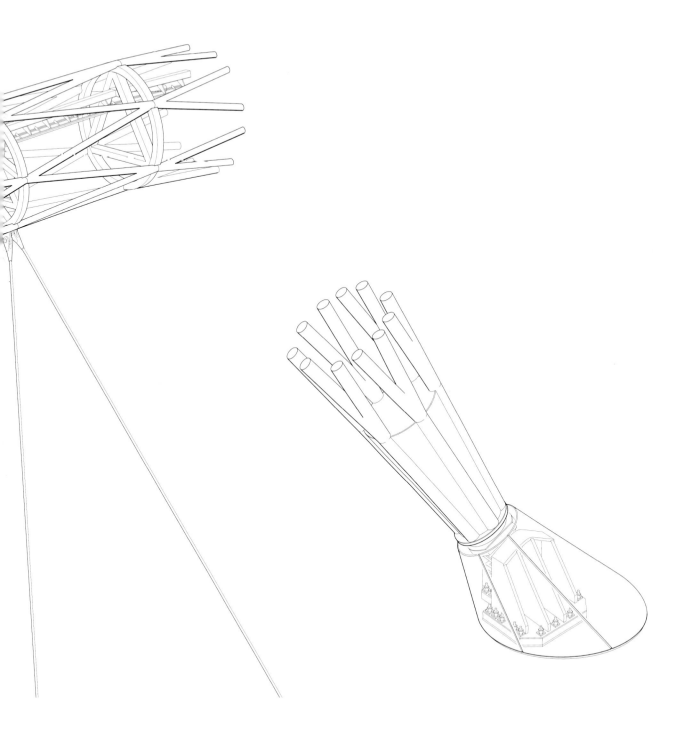

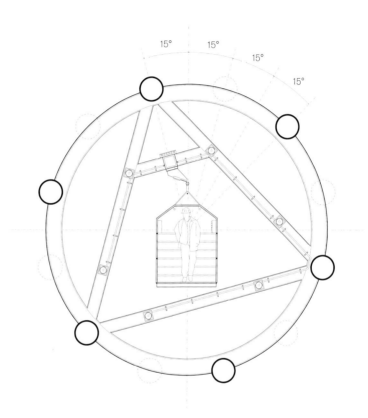

15° 15° 15° 15°

Left: A detail of the arch and the suspension cables that support the stadium's roof.

Above: A typical cross-section through the arch; the structure is 7.4 metres in diameter – wide enough for a train to pass through.

Facts and figures

Wembley Stadium
    London, England
    1996–2007
Client
    Wembley National Stadium Ltd
Architects
    World Stadium Team (Foster +
    Partners, HOK Sport and LOBB
    Partnership)
Project Team (Foster + Partners)
    Norman Foster
    Mouzhan Majidi
    Alistair Lenczner
    Huw Thomas
    Angus Campbell
    Ken Shuttleworth
    Richard Hawkins
    Zak Ayash
    Juan Frigerio
    Tony Miki
    Carlo Negri
    Pearl Tang
    Colin Ward
    Vincent Westbrook
    Dion Young

    Nathan Barr
    David Goss
    Trevore Grams
    Edward Highton
    Phyllis Fat Yin Lam
    Richard Locke
    Eyal Nir
    Erik Ramelow
    Horacio Schmidt

    Jonathan Scull
    Chee Huang Seah
    James Speed
    James Thomas
    Wing Sai Tsui
    Andrew Wood

Project Team (HOK Sport/LOBB
Partnership)
    Rod Sheard
    Ben Vickery
    Megan Ashfield
    Richard Breslin
    Warrick Chalmers
    Dale Jennings
    David Manica
    Alastair Pope

Consultants
    Structural and Civil Engineer:
    Mott Stadium Consortium
    Mechanical and Electrical Engineer:
    Mott Stadium Consortium
    Cost Consultant: Franklin +
    Andrews
    Disabled Access Consultant: Sinclair
    Knight Merz (Europe) Ltd
    Transport and Crowd Movement:
    Steer Davis Gleave
    Pitch Consultant: Sports Turf
    Research Institute
    Planning Consultant: Nathaniel
    Lichfield and Partners
    Planning Supervisor: Arup
    Catering Consultant: Mike Driscoll
    & Associates

    Signage: Identica
    Main Contractor: Multiplex

Principal Awards
    2007 Vodafone Live Music Awards,
    Best Live Music Venue
    2008 LABC National Built in Quality
    Awards – Overall Winner
    2008 LABC National Built in Quality
    Awards – Best Commercial Project
    2008 World Architecture Festival
    – High Commendation, Sport
    2008 RIBA National Award
    2008 RIBA Award
    2008 London District Surveyors
    Association Quality Awards, Best
    Commercial Project
    2008 London District Surveyors
    Association Quality Awards, Best
    Structural Innovation

Project chronology

1922 Construction of Wembley Stadium begins; designed by Sir John Simpson and Maxwell Ayrton, and engineered by Sir Owen Williams, it is constructed in just 300 days. The stadium forms the centrepiece of the Empire Exhibition and has a capacity of 120,000 spectators

1923 28 April: the first FA Cup Final between Bolton Wanderers and West Ham United; Bolton win 2–0, but the match is marred by 200,000 people (rather than the anticipated 120,000) turning up to watch, the crowd spilling on to the pitch

1924 12 April: the first international match in the stadium, England draws 1–1 with Scotland
23 April: the Empire Exhibition is opened by King George V; the largest exhibition ever staged anywhere in the world it attracts 27 million visitors

1925 31 October: the Empire Exhibition closes

1948 Wembley hosts the major track events of the XIV Olympiad; London had been granted the 1944 event but this was not staged due to the Second World War

1953 2 May: the 'Matthews Final', supposedly the greatest FA Cup Final at Wembley; Blackpool win 4–3 against Bolton Wanderers
25 November: Hungary becomes the first foreign team to win at Wembley, beating England 6–3

1954 16 April: Billy Graham hosts a Christian 'crusade' in front of 120,000 people

1955 Floodlighting is introduced to the stadium

1960 England are named as hosts of the 1966 World Cup, with the final to be staged at Wembley

1963 18 June: Cooper v Clay World Heavyweight non-title fight; Clay beats Cooper in the fifth round
A new fixed roof is installed above the seating area

1966 30 July: England beats West Germany 4–2 after extra time in the final to win the World Cup; Geoff Hurst scores a hat trick

1972 5 August: the London Rock and Roll Show, the first pop concert at Wembley features Bill Haley, Little Richard and Billy Fury

1982 29 May: Pope John Paul II celebrates mass at the stadium

1985 13 July: the Live Aid concert is held at the stadium

1990 16 April: the Nelson Mandela Tribute concert for a free South Africa is held to celebrate his release after twenty-eight years in jail

1998 Wembley plc sells Wembley Stadium to the FA for £120 million; the FA creates a subsidiary company, Wembley National Stadium Ltd (WNSL), to run the stadium and prepare for its rebuilding

1999 29 July: the scheme for the new stadium is launched; the stadium has a masted structure to support the retractable roof
31 July–3 August: Norman Foster redesigns the scheme; the masts are abandoned in favour of an arch

2000 7 October: England's last match in the old stadium; Germany beats England 1–0; Dietmar Hamann of Germany scores the last ever goal there
1 June: planning permission is granted for the new Wembley Stadium; it is designed by the World Stadium Team (WST), a partnership between Foster + Partners and HOK Sport/LOBB Partnership (now known as Populous)

2002	30 September: demolition of the old stadium begins
2003	7 February: the twin towers are demolished – the last elements of the old stadium to fall Piling for the foundations of the new stadium commences; the piles go down as far as 35 metres – as deep as the twin towers were tall
2004	24 June: the Wembley arch reaches its final position, 133 metres above the pitch
2006	The projected opening of the stadium, in time for the FA Cup Final in May 2006, is postponed 19 June: the turf is complete
2007	9 March: the new stadium is complete and handed over to the FA 17 March: the stadium is open for public viewing by local residents; it hosts a series of warm-up events during March and April 11 May: the statue of Bobby Moore outside the stadium entrance is unveiled by Sir Bobby Charlton 19 May: the first FA Cup Final is staged in the new stadium; Chelsea beats Manchester 1–0

Vital statistics

Site area
   500,000 square metres

Building area (gross)
   170,000 square metres

Building area (net)
   120,000 square metres hospitality accommodation

Overall dimensions
   300 metres east-west
   280 metres north-south
   49 metres from main concourse to top of roof

Number of floors
   Eight

Seating capacity
   There are three seating tiers, the lower tier holding 34,303 spectators, the middle tier 16,532, and the upper tier 39,165 – a total of 90,000 seats for football and rugby events; there would be 68,400 to 72,000 for athletics events

Budget shell and core
   £350 million

Cost per seat
   Approximately £3,900

Arch
   The arch structure has a span of 315 metres, a height of 133 metres and weighs 1,750 tonnes, making it the largest clear-span stadium roof structure in the world

   The arch leans asymmetrically to the north, at 68 degrees to the horizontal, clear from the path of the moving roof panels on the south east and west sides

   The arch structure is 7.4 metres in diameter – wide enough for a train to pass through

Root
   Partially retractable, large-span roof suspended below the arch; in the closed position the roof covers all 90,000 seats; the roof panels can open or close fully within an hour

   With the roof in retracted position, late spring matches such as the FA Cup Final can be played on a sunlit pitch for better spectator viewing

Hospitality
   Hospitality facilities are concentrated on the north side of the stadium from where 70 per cent of people typically arrive

The function rooms and catering facilities on the concourses include twelve restaurants ranging from 500 to 2,000 seats; together they provide 15,000 seated meal covers per event, including capacity for 2,000 guests in London's largest banqueting hall

There are 98 kitchens, the largest being one third the size of the pitch; there are 5,000 catering staff on major event days. There are 688 refreshment points, compared with 152 in the old stadium

There are 17,500 Club Wembley hospitality seats, including 156 boxes, which are rented for ten years at a time according to a three-tier system: gold, silver and bronze

Spectator amenities
The stadium includes a high-quality sound PA system which can be used as part of concert sound system

The angle of the terraces is steeper than in the old stadium bowl with a maximum rake of 34 degrees at the back of the upper tier

The seating bowl geometry includes curved terracing plan on all sides to optimise viewing within the stadium; all spectators have unobstructed sightlines

Each spectator seat space is a minimum of 500 x 800mm: 30 per cent more than in the old stadium

All spectators can use escalators to travel to the upper tiers
Over 300 dedicated viewing positions for disabled spectators are distributed between all levels

There are 2,600 toilets, 150 of which allow disabled access

Stadium back-of-house
Pedestrian circulation at concourse level is segregated from stadium operations in the basement, which includes a 360-degree service road, loading bays and storage spaces

The vehicle compound in the basement can accommodate all TV outside broadcast and production trucks, away from public areas

A comprehensive security suite monitors activity in all parts of the stadium

Pitch
The natural grass pitch is orientated east-west as in the old stadium

There are 107 steps from the pitch up to the Royal Box, situated at the front of the middle tier

Athletics Configuration
The conversion from football to athletics configuration takes approximately ten weeks, during which time the temporary platform structure is built and the athletics track laid
The athletics arena created complies with all IAAF technical requirements for Category 1 events. The heavy-duty platform structure is built using a prefabricated modular steel system. International standard football can still be played on a pitch installed on the temporary platform

Transport connections
The stadium is located close to two London Underground stations: Wembley Park and Wembley Central – and one mainline railway station: Wembley Stadium

100 trains an hour arrive in the vicinity of Wembley on a major event day; these combined allow all 90,000 spectators to arrive at the stadium by public transport

No specific public car-parking provision is made

Credits

Editor: David Jenkins
Design: Thomas Manss
& Company; Thomas Manss,
Tom Featherby, Angela
Pescolderung
Picture Research:
Gayle Mault, Lauren Catten
Proofreading: Julia Dawson,
Rebecca Roke
Production Supervision:
Martin Lee, John Bodkin
Reproduction: DawkinsColour
Printed and bound in Italy
by Grafiche SiZ SpA.

The FSC®-certified paper
GardaMatt has been supplied
by Cartiere del Garda SpA, Italy

FSC
www.fsc.org
MIX
Paper from
responsible sources
FSC® C005613

Picture credits

Photographs
Action Images: 31 (bottom), 68,
69
Art Archive: 15 (top)
Bettmann Archive/Corbis: 22
(top)
Richard Davies: 58
Foster + Partners: 33, 39, 70-71
Getty Images: 14 (l, r), 15
(bottom), 17 (top, bottom), 22
(middle), 26-27, 30 (bottom)
Hulton Archive/Getty: 25 (top)
Keystone: 20-21
National Archives Image Library:
23 (bottom)
Picture Post: 23 (top)
Popperfoto: 16, 22 (bottom), 24
(top, bottom), 25 (bottom), 28, 30
(top)
Rex Features/Nigel Barklie: 31
(top)
Rex Features/Nils Jorgensen: 29
Nigel Young/Foster + Partners:
6-7, 42, 43, 45, 46, 47, 52-53,
59, 60, 61, 62, 63, 66-67, 74, 75,
76, 77, 78-79, 80, 81, 82-83, 86,
88-89, 94-95

Drawings and Visualisations
Birds Portchmouth Russum: 40,
41, 72-73
Norman Foster: 4, 5, 37
Foster + Partners: 18, 19, 34, 35,
36, 38, 44, 48, 49, 50-51, 54, 55,
56, 57, 64-65
Gregory Gibbon/Foster +
Partners: 12-13, 84-85, 87

Every effort has been made
to contact copyright holders.
The publishers apologise for
any omissions which they will
be pleased to rectify at the
earliest opportunity.

Editor's Note

In editing this book I am
particularly grateful to Norman
Foster and Simon Inglis for their
invaluable contributions. I would
also like to thank Thomas Manss
and Tom Featherby for bringing
the book to life graphically; Gayle
Mault and Lauren Catten, who
together mined the office archive;
Julia Dawson and Rebecca
Roke for proofreading the text;
Martin Lee and John Bodkin
for coordinating production;
and the numerous people in
the Foster studio who helped to
piece together the background
to the project.

David Jenkins
London, June 2012